I *Almost*
GAVE UP...

Until I *Realized*
Giving up
Wasn't an Option...

DR. "P.J." MCPHEE

I *Almost*

GAVE UP...

Until I *Realized* Giving up Wasn't an Option...

I Almost Gave Up... Until I Realized Giving Up Wasn't an Option...

Printed in the United States of America
ISBN 978-1-967279-38-8 (hc)
ISBN 978-1-967279-37-1 (sc)
ISBN 978-1-967279-39-5 (e)

06.10.2025

This book is printed on acid-free paper.

The contents of this work, including, but not limited to, the accuracy of events, people, and places depicted; opinions expressed; permission to use previously published materials included; and any advice given or actions advocated are solely the responsibility of the author, who assumes all liability for said work and indemnifies the publisher against any claims stemming from publication of the work.

Blue Ink Media Solutions
1111B S Governors Ave
STE 7582 Dover,
DE 19904

www.blueinkmediasolutions.com

TABLE OF CONTENTS

Dedication

How can you script reality? I searched Webster's Dictionary and Thesaurus from A through Z to find another word for "gratitude" and "appreciation" and could not come up with anything but "Thank You." Thanks to God for His many blessings; thanks to family members who were so supportive; thanks to friends who were there when I needed them to be editors and offered strong encouragement and assistance; and most of all, to my husband Willis, who continued to pray and support me without ceasing.

This book is for you.

Am I in Heaven?

OH MY GOD! Am I dead? And better yet, if I am dead, am I in Heaven? I see this tall white female with outstretched hands dressed in all white, with long hair down to the end of her spine smiling at me. I'm nervous and feel myself getting anxious with anticipation. What's going on?God, please don't let me be dead! I have not seen my two girls grow up and get their families.

I am too young, God, to die. I don't even have any grandbabies yet. Then as this young angel walks towards me with this South African dialect (as I wonder what part of heaven I am in), I hear a voice saying, "Mrs. McPhee, are you awake? I need you to open your eyes and wake up. The procedure is over and you did well!"

Then it hit me! I had just gone through a surgery and was waking up just in time to see my friend Sherry standing there.

You see, Sherry is a friend I had just met at a Lifestyle Center, and I was all alone from home and had to have emergency surgery. She was off from work at the time and I later found out that she had stayed with me all that night. I was so glad to see her because I live in Florida, and I was in the hospital in Tennessee with no family or friends and needless to say, I was terrified. But even better than that, I was glad to see that I was not dead.

Several months prior to this, I had a miscarriage and it was determined that some of the fetus had been left inside me, so for months I walked around with toxic poisoning and did not know it. I literally felt

1

as if I was dying. I could not walk very well and the room was always spinning. I had a metallic taste in my mouth all the time and could not figure out why. While at the Lifestyle Center, my husband and children came to visit, but it was determined (after they left) that I needed surgery. I think that was about surgery number 16 or 17?? Oh yeah, about this time I had already had multiple surgeries. I had a lot of time to think while recuperating. My mind went so many different places and I began to question my belief and relationship with God, and then I began to try to psychoanalyze God. I felt He could have done a better job than what He was doing. Certainly He had gone to sleep or something when it came to my life.

What could be going on in my life so wrong? Here I am, a young woman who gave her life to Christ at an early age. My father is a pastor of a large congregation and I have done nothing but work in the church. Not to mention, I forgot to tell you that I'm a PK (Preacher's Kid). I grew up in a Pentecostal church where we had to be at church 24/7, it seemed at the time. I sang in the Gospel Angels' Choir when I wanted to and when I didn't want to. Church was our life! All of our friends were close because we were all in the same boat! Stuck at church alllll the time. I saw my other siblings (who shall remain nameless to protect the innocent) do just about whatever they wanted to do after they moved away from home. But no, I stayed in the church. And now I'm looking at them and one of them had the nerve to call me yesterday (don't worry, Victor, I'm not telling anyone it was you) and tell me how good God had been to me and He was just thinking about me and my situation and it amazes him how I hang in there.

He is the biggest devil of them all, and now he was praying for me?? Well you can only imagine what I told him. PLEASE stop praying for me! Maybe that's why I'm having such a hard time. I have a baby sister whom I beg and PAY not to pray for me. For some reason these siblings of mine feel as though our parents are Christians and that is enough for them.

Take, for instance, we were in church one Tuesday night, this is youth night at church and we had a revival. You know in the Pentecostal church we got saved every revival. So Babro, my brother, was tired because he was in school that day skipping class. He made a hole in the ceiling and was up there all day just cutting class. I think he may have been suspended so that's why he had to hide. But anyway, the ceiling collapsed and you guessed it right. He came tumbling down and scared everyone in the class. He was covered with white ash from head to toe, looking around as if everyone else was at fault.

The teacher called the principal and he came in and escorted him right off to the office. OK, so you know the rest of the story with that. Well that night during church service, he said he wanted to do the right things and he wasn't sure why he stayed in trouble all the time, but he had made the decision to change. Well of course the saints were saying "Praise God" and were glad another teenager was considering salvation. You would think by now they would have noticed how all of us got saved over and over again. They didn't care. They just wanted us to come as many times as it took. So Babro was on the altar saying "Jesus, please help me," and one of the mothers of the church said, "That's right, just ask Him into your heart." They sang and sang and sang. By this time I knew what was going on. They said we are going to stay here with him if it takes all night. I said to myself, I am not staying all night with this foolishness. He had already said earlier what his plan was to prevent him from getting in so much trouble about the ceiling. So I went over to the altar to pretend to be praying and what do I hear? Snoring! This joker is on the altar asleep, with slob all over his face. I pinched him and said, "Boy, if you don't get up. You got all these people thinking you trying to get salvation and find Jesus and you are asleep." So he raises his head slowly and peeps around. Well, he is the only person still on their knees so he has to play the role. He jumps up as if he feels something like he got saved. They always ask you to testify and tell how different you feel. I was shaking my head and saying, God, please don't strike him dead on the altar 'cause he looks like he's fixing to make up a good one. So it was already late and they grabbed him by the arm and he headed for the pew and pretended to be so anointed that he couldn't speak. Go figure! But anyways, getting back to the point!

So I had time to think about some of the things I had gone through, so many times I wanted to throw in the towel and give up, but God wouldn't let me. I am sharing this testimony just in case there is someone who is also thinking about giving up. I wanted to give up, but like a songwriter said, "I looked around and I thought things over," and I realized that I had overcoming abilities, and that the good did outweigh the bad.

Right before I visited the Lifestyle Center, around midnight, I had a VERY bad anxiety attack. Didn't know what was going on, but I felt I was going to die. I called my parents because they lived only about three blocks from me, and I was home alone because my husband and daughters were in Fort Lauderdale at a church basketball game. I was nervous and things were not right in my head. I was out of control so they called 911 and the paramedics came to transport me to the hospital. I was on the stretcher facing the door and I could see in the reflection of the window of the door, one of the paramedics with his hand to his head in a circular motion telling the other paramedics I was "Cuckoo." I could see him so clearly but I was petrified to say anything. The first thing that came to mind was that if I confronted him he could do anything to me. But the best thing about the situation was that the other men in the ambulance observed the fact that I was watching and they were sympathetic, so I didn't let his ignorance bother me too much. At least for a minute I was focusing on him and not the problem I was experiencing. I guess some good did come out of the situation! It was later determined that I had some side effects from Levaquin, an antibiotic which causes hallucinations in some patients.

One of my best memories was when I was about 14 years old trying to get into this Junior Sorority Club and everyone just sitting around the patio. I had to go to the restroom so I got up and opened the sliding door. Then I feel this awful pain on my forehead and blood rolling down my face, only to find out the sliding door was already open and I closed it and ran right into it. What did that have to do with anything? Nothing! I just thought about it.

I did not keep a record of these events and I'm writing from memory, so you will find me going back and forth in time. Don't worry if you get a little confused. It's my story and I'm confused already myself.

Baby Stories

ONE COOL JANUARY day, I was sick with chills and fever and felt really terrible. And after taking over-the-counter medication for the flu and not getting any better, I decided to go to the doctor only to find out it was not the flu, but I was pregnant.

As the doctor was speaking to me, I began to cry. You see, I had already had three miscarriages and the doctor had warned me about getting pregnant again. The procedure to make sure I did not have any more children was scheduled in about six weeks. The doctor said, "You have two choices. Either we can terminate the pregnancy now, or just wait for your body to do so, but I don't recommend that," he said. So I told him I would think about it and get back with him quickly. After having prayer with my parents and church members, it was decided that I would just let God work it out however He saw fit. Well as time moved on, I had some complications of course, but for the most part, the pregnancy was fine. Until in the seventh month when I got a very bad sore throat, that is. The doctor had warned me about taking over- the-counter medication, so I telephoned his office and he said even though it was only a sore throat, he wanted to see me. My mom and I were going to the mall later on that day so we were riding together and she drove me to the doctor's office first. He checked my throat and the most peculiar thing had happened. My throat stopped hurting, so I told him I was fine and I would see him on next week at my regular scheduled visit. Then he paused and said, "Well while you are here I might as well examine you." Of course going to the mall was the only thing on my mind at the time, and I did feel okay, but he insisted. So I had the examination and he calmly said, "Something is wrong with my ultrasound machine so I need you to go over to the hospital to have the test done over there." So I didn't think anything was wrong; I just told my mom that I had to go over to the hospital to have a test done and that it was still on the way to the mall. Well I got in the car, and my mom was driving like a race-car driver. I looked and asked, "What in the world is your problem?" She was just singing and praying and trying to remain calm, but I thought she was just driving fast to get me to the appointment so we could get the sale at Burdines and JC Penney. I was saying to myself, goodness, she is really trying to get me there. By the time I could ask any more questions we were going into the emergency room entrance and there were doctors and nurses pulling on me so fast, putting me on a stretcher, snatching off my clothes, and I'm saying what in the world is going on? By the time they did this the doctor was coming around the corner and said the baby was not breathing and in distress and that he had to take him right away. He said he had already told my mom not to tell me because the stress would cause greater danger for the baby. I said to myself, she gets an "A" for today because she did an excellent job keeping her mouth closed. I had an early delivery and the baby was underweight, but they said, "Look, you have a healthy bouncing baby girl. She is so pretty."

"What, a girl? I couldn't be hearing you right after you have told me for seven months I was having a boy and I have nothing but boy clothes!"

"A Girl! Oh my goodness; A Girl!" My mom said, "You might as well calm down and hold this baby 'cause she is here and there is no exchanging." I finally held her and was wondering how that little blue boy sailor suit would look on her. Just kidding.

After awhile she was allowed to come home and she was still jaundiced so the doctor told me to make sure she got plenty of sun. So here I am walking around inside the house looking for sun. I would find a place, lay her down, and as soon as I laid her down the sun would move.

So I'm already paranoid and frantic being a new mother; I'm worried that she is not going to get any better or get enough sun. So I kept on looking inside because it was windy outside and we could not go out. I walked and was almost in tears just praying that the sun would remain long enough for my baby to get the sunlight she needed. Well long story short, my mom came into the room and asked, "What in the world is your problem, running around the house with the baby searching for the sun?" She told me to lay the baby down and assured me she would be all right. She said I was probably doing more harm running around the house than not having the sun. It is funny now, but it definitely was not funny at the time. Only to go to the mailbox and get her birth certificate to find out that someone had made a BIG mistake. At birth the name given was Zylandria Delores W. Well, but when the birth certificate came back it said Zylandria Delores Amen W. I screamed so loud! How can they make such a stupid mistake? My father, the pastor, told me not to have it changed, that an angel might have put it there and that it was a tremendous blessing. He said it was a good reason it was done and that it would be all right. Well people started to call her "Amen," and I got weary that she would grow up to hate me for that. So I told her that I had three miscarriages and God allowed her to live and that she was not breathing for a long period of time. As I looked back during that time, I could not remember her moving for days or weeks. God had given us a miracle delivery and I stressed what a Blessing she was, so I think she accepted it. (I am good.)

She was about three months old and we attended a women's conference. It was that Sunday and we all met after checking out of the hotel in the lobby. Just standing around getting ready to leave when one of the maids asked if we had everything and was everything OK? Well of course we're looking at each other and wondering what she's talking about when she said, "Well if you have everything I guess no one knows who left the baby upstairs," and before she could finish the sentence you just see crazy women running to the elevators and stairs as if we had lost our minds. I asked my mom, "How could you leave my only child?" She said, "Easy, the same way you left your only child, but you're worse than I am. She is your child!" Yes it's funny now again, but it was not funny at the time. But believe it or not, I was going to run some errands a few months later and I had my niece Yva in the car with me, and as we drove down the street, she asked, "Auntie, what did ZeeZee do so bad that you left her home?" I turned around on two wheels and drove on two wheels all the way back home. Well years later I told this to ZeeZee and she asked, "For crying out loud, what kind of mother are you? You forget me not once but twice in a lifetime."

Around the age of four she got up for breakfast and asked for some pancakes from McDonald's. I told her I did not feel like driving to McDonald's and that she would have to eat whatever was at home. She tells me she is going to have morning prayer and during the prayer she asks God for some pancakes because He can do anything. I opened my eyes during the prayer and said to myself, you can pray to whomever, I am not going to McDonald's this day. She went around the house just singing and praying and I said to myself, what if I don't get her the pancakes? That may cause her not to have any faith in God and in prayer. Now I'm confused because I'm second-guessing myself. Oh she prayed and prayed until I really felt guilty. I said, "Come on, girl, let's go to McDonald's." When we got to the window she told the lady she had prayed for the pancakes and she hoped they were going to be good because God gave her these pancakes. I was so excited that she was praying that when my husband came home I told him and all he said was, "Pee, I don't believe you. You just got played by a baby." I stood there for the longest time trying to figure out what really had happened.

When she was about ten, she started to pray and ask for a sister. This is a child that prayed all the time and talked about dreams she had praying for people. We would drive by and she would see someone who was begging for food and throw money out to them. One day we went to Denny's Restaurant to eat and a lady had a little girl and they did not have enough money, so ZeeZee paid the bill. So I get a little weary when she starts to pray. I'm already tired and DON'T want any more children and am begging God to ignore her in a mighty way. So one day at the church, there was a little two- month-old girl whose mother had a little situation and the maternal grandmother was taking care of the other three siblings and a sick son, whom Hospice had given only about a week or so to live. So the grandmother had her hands full so ZeeZee asked if we could keep the baby she had been praying for. Well I quickly assured her this was not the baby she was praying for, and I made it perfectly clear that we could only help out for one night. I had not even spoken to my husband about it, so now I had to do some praying. Zee said it would be all right because this was the baby she had prayed for, and God was going to make it all right. We got home with the baby and Zee begged my husband Willis to keep the baby for a night and he agreed. I was surprised that he agreed so quickly, so we took the baby in and cared for her, went shopping, and were having a good time. But then I thought that we might be making a mistake because we had to give the baby back and we didn't want to get too attached. So the next day we found the grandmother and Hospice was there and the other siblings were there and things were really chaotic, so the grandmother asked if we could keep her another night. It was fine with Zee and me, but the problem was, we were leaving the next day to go to St. Augustine for a family vacation, and I just knew my husband was not taking an infant with us. So when he got home the baby was still there. He said, "I see you did not take the baby back!" And Zee jumped up in his lap and said, "Yes we did, but we had to bring her back because the grandmother would not take her." I told him immediately about the chaos and how we were doing missionary work. He looked and shook his head. Well that one night turned into two nights and two nights turned into a weekend, and the weekend turned into eleven years later when she is a permanent part of this family. The baby was born with a hole in her heart and asthma, but she is healthy now and striving quite well. She had three surgeries by the time she was two years old, but thanks to God who is a healer, she is doing wonderful. Dominique is a VERY talented young girl and a Blessing to the family. She will soon be one of the greatest pianists of all time. She is a very tall, pretty little girl who has a beautiful voice, and she can play volleyball. She is a great student in school and shows God how much she appreciates what He has done in her life by being a good person.

After reading this book you are going to think I have ADHD or autism or something, but I promise you I am sane (kind of). One night Zee brings Dominique to the kitchen, where I was frantic. Zee says, "Look at this hard bump on Dominique's breast." I run over to Dominique and feel her breast and there is this hard bump on her. I already told you she was born with health issues. I grabbed her and asked if it hurt and she said no. Then I frantically start drilling her with questions like, "How long has it been there?" "Why didn't you let me know earlier?" and so on. I called my mom, and by this time I'm in tears and have diagnosed her with breast cancer with only a few months to live. I put her in the car and ran to my parents' home, and my mom and niece are looking as if I had lost my mind and simply said, "I think it's only her breast just starting to grow." I couldn't remember that ever happening to me or to Zee, so I asked Zee and she said she couldn't remember, and my mom reminded me that I was over 50 years old and that's why I couldn't remember that far back. Well that was not good enough; my physician just happens to belong to my church, so when I got to church he was not there but his wife was. So I apologized (upfront) for dragging her into the restroom to look at Dominique and her 12-year-old daughter was with her, and she tried really hard not to laugh in my face, but it was her daughter that said, "Yes, this happened to me too. She is just starting to get breast." I couldn't understand why it would be on just one side but oh well, I could go back into church feeling stupid but relieved.

Another baby story is when Yva (my niece) was born. I was in the birthing room with my sister Buffy and the midwife. I was the coach for the delivery, so I was deep breathing and the whole nine yards. Buffy was fine and didn't really have too many complaints. At times it really didn't seem as if she was even in labor. Things were getting close and I was being a champ. Yva was coming out and I was excited UNTIL the midwife pulled out a clamp, which looked like a large pair of pliers, to pull the baby's head out. Well that's where they lost me. I saw the head and started sweating and shaking so the nurse started to pull off my shirt to cool me off with a cold towel. They were just working on me to revive me when I heard this faint voice call out, "Hey, did you guys forget me? Forget her; I'm the one having a baby." They dragged me on out of the way and started to finish delivering the baby. She came out with a smooched-up face and head, but thank God for prayer. The nurse said, "I know this baby's got a headache." But then she realized no one was smiling at that sad joke, so she said, "All you have to do is rub her head softly and shape it and she will be all right." Okay, Yva, Auntie loves her smooch-faced firstborn.

Horse Hair for Ears

I'**M GOING TO** take you back some years when I was about seventeen years old. Our family was on vacation driving from Florida to Canada to visit Niagara Falls for my graduation. We were having a good time traveling and sightseeing, so we stopped to go into the mall. Buffy, my baby sister, was only about six years old at the time and you know how you see the little booths in the mall; well Buffy wanted to have her ears pierced. So Mom tells her to go ask Dad, and she came running back to where I was and told me he told her yes. Okay! Now you tell me, do you think I was wrong to go and have mine done also? Remember she is about six years old and I am seventeen. My dad had been telling me all these years that I could not have my ears pierced, so being the good child that I was, I never questioned it. Lo and behold when we got back to the van, he looks at me with this weird look on his face and starts to yell at me. So the first thing that comes to my mind is that he has lost his cotton-picking mind. How can he tell a six-year-old she can have her ears pierced and tell me no. So I stand there and wait for an apology, and the man walks off. "Oh no he didn't!" I said (to myself of course).

So I was in tears and we had an aunt with us and she just tried her best to console me, but I was still just so convinced that my dad had turned into Jekyll and Mr. Hyde. So my mom came back and said my dad told her that during prayer one day when I was younger, the Lord told him I was never supposed to have my ears pierced or I would have problems with it. Well you know what my next question is! Why in the Sam and eggs didn't he tell me this? And you already know the rest of the story. Yes, keloids as large as strawberries grew very rapidly on my ears. You know how the old folk used homemade remedies. So there was this old lady who was like the medicine woman of remedies in the neighborhood. She had the answer to the problem, or so she thought. She told me to get some horse hair and bring it to her, and she was very specific with the type of horse hair to get. I, along with a dear friend of mine, went out on the farm, found a poor horse, and I explained to the horse that I needed the hair more than he did, and that it would grow back. I didn't think talking to the horse was any crazier than us out there pulling his hair. Anyway! OK, my dear friend, did you notice I didn't put your name in this?? I took all the blame for it, so you don't have to worry because I'm not telling anyone you were with me and that this was your idea.

The process was to tie the horse hair around the keloids. Just for the record back then they were not called "keloids," they were called "titties." For the next however long I would have to go back and let her continue to tighten them, and the titties would eventually fall off. Okay, don't act like you don't know this was barbaric and painful. Time went on and yes, I looked crazy trying to wear hairstyles and hats to hide both the titties and the horsehair.

Until one day somebody in the house had a Re-ve-la-tion to take me to the doctor. A REAL Physician! I guess by now my mom stepped in to help after I had made a mess of things. I went into the office, and he saw it and said, "What in the world is that?" I said to myself, your guess is as good as mine. Mom gave me the eye, and I knew better than to tell that man what had really happened 'cause it was no doubt in my mind that the Department of Children and Families would be called. So it was determined that he had to surgically remove them. I said okay, anything beats that horsehair. So a date was scheduled. The surgeon, who shall remain nameless, cut the entire earlobes off. Yes I did look crazy and deformed, and then the keloids grew back.

I don't know how because I did not have an earlobe, so apparently they created themselves a new earlobe and grew themselves back. He was confused and apparently did not know any more than the little old lady with the horsehair. Eventually, after about three more surgeries, another surgeon was able to remove them and build me more earlobes. Now I'm warning you, DO NOT come around me staring at my ears trying to see how my earlobes look. My ears are fine now and I have never needed another surgery. All praise belongs to God.

How to Get a Whipping

I **WAS FOR** the most part a pretty good child. I didn't get into much trouble because I did not like to be disciplined and/or punished. My brothers got whippings EVERY DAY. One day I heard Babro saying to Marvin, "You know, I haven't gotten a whipping today." So they were really experts when it came to getting whippings or being on punishment. That was back in the 1970s before the abuse hotline and when anyone in the neighborhood or church could whip you.

One Sunday after church we were at the kitchen table having dinner and we had string beans. I just could not seem to get string beans down for anything in the world. But we had strawberry shortcake for dessert, and if you didn't eat your vegetables you could not have dessert. The chair next to me was empty so I put the string beans in a napkin and folded it and when Mom looked she said, "Good job, now you can have dessert." Well technically I didn't lie because I never said I ate the stupid beans. She assumed I did because she did not see them. Then there is a knock at the door, and it is one of the sisters from the church stopping by. Mom asked if she wanted some dinner, and I was praying in the Spirit that she said no because the only chair empty was the one with the string beans and Mom was standing there so I could not move them. So she said no! Boy, sweat was coming from every part of my body. That wasn't good enough for my mom. "Oh come on, Sister Butler, and sit down right here." Now I forgot to mention to you it was the first Sunday, and the church had communion and Sister Butler had on white from the top of her head to the soles of her feet.

Yeah you guessed it, she sat down and string bean stains all over Sister Butler's crispy white dress. I started speaking in an unknown tongue and asking God to accept me into the kingdom because I knew my mom was getting ready to take me out of this world. I had seen her whipping my brothers and I knew she knew how to handle the belt. Sister Butler pleaded for my mom not to beat me, but my mom looked at me with the "eye" and I knew I was out for the count. My brother said, "Stupid girl, you should have paid me to eat the beans for you or just given them to me under the table." He said, "It's going to be worse on you because you are not used to getting whippings like us." She made me get up from the dinner table and go into the room. It was Sunday and she felt holy, so I guess she was saving the whipping for later. That was the worst feeling in the world, to let whippings and punishments pile up. So Babro came in and said, "But all you have to do is lay on the bed and start kicking your legs real hard. Move from side-to- side, front-to-back, it's a rhythm." He said it would confuse her and she would get tired trying to keep up with you. He said he had another rhythm but she broke the code, but this one was new and she hadn't caught on yet. So he had me lay on the bed and practice, and while I was practicing Mom came in for something but she was laughing sooo hard until all she could do was walk out.

My brother started clowning around and she laughed even more. Then he told me later on how much I owed him for saving me from my whipping. I was very grateful to my brother for all his help, so I wanted to do something nice for him. I knew he had not fed his little fish he got from the fair, so I did it for him. I fed the fish Lay's potato chips and you know the rest of the story. He came in and found the little critters floating on the top of the greasy water. And no, I was not crazy enough to confess, because my mom owed me a punishment and I did not want her to remember Sister Butler's white dress.

She used to say all the time, "All right, I'm paying you for the old and new." Now as we have grown up we realize it was just a ploy to keep us in check and it worked. We had a little funeral for the fish and my brother went on being bad as usual. Speaking of bad, this is the same brother who was wrestling with me and broke my fingernails. I had grown these very nice fingernails and it took me forever to grow them, and he was just annoying and broke them. Well I scratched him and yanked his mouth and ran into my parents' bedroom. They were not at home of course and I locked the door.

Well this crazy boy broke down the door like he was James Bond or someone and I was stupid and called the police. The officer came out and boy did I regret it. He gave us this lecture on how delinquent we were to call 911, which is for emergencies only, wasting his time when he could have been out helping someone who really needed him. He warned us not to ever do it again. You would think that punishment was enough, right? Wrong! Sister "Hit them with your best shot" found out, yes Mom, and I would have rather gone with the police officer. After our one-on-one contact, believe me I never again tried that.

While I am on this brother, let me tell you about how he burst open his back and needed stitches and how we tried to stitch him with needle and thread. Well this was back in the days when children knew how to play like children. We would meet on a regular basis to one of our relatives' homes in the projects. This time we just happened to be at Aunt Nathalie's home jumping over lawn chairs. There were at least 20 cousins each time we played because there were so many of us. The Roshers, Greens, Freemans, Houstons, Dampiers and so forth, to name a few, and we also had friends like the Andersons, Gambles, and Pressleys. No one outside the loop wanted to ever fight one of us because they already knew they had to fight the group.

Well Babro, of course, just had to be the competitor all the time. He just had to be the best at whatever we did and Tree and Ruthie (our cousins) were his cheerleaders. We jumped over chairs for hours and laughed and played when Ruthie convinced him to stack up some more chairs and jump. Needless to say, he found delight in the idea. So they stacked the chairs and he jumped and after the challenge was gone, they stacked more chairs and the nutcase decided to jump. Sure he made it, but he came down so hard on his back and all we heard was

"Momma!!" You guessed it. He busted his back open and all we saw was blood everywhere. His cheerleaders Tree and Ruthie were the first to run screaming, but then they got themselves together and tried to find towels and sheets to help. Well we knew he needed stitches, but he didn't want to go to the hospital so we felt we could stitch him up with some thread and needle. That was not a good idea. A friend of ours, Latonya, called her mom (who, by the way, was a real nurse), and she stitched him up.

That didn't stop him because as soon as he got well, he found something else stupid to do. Like one day he had on a towel for a cape to be Superman. There was some construction going on in the neighborhood, and there were these large underground sewer pipes on the side of the road waiting to be put down. You guessed it again. He had some boys roll a large pipe towards him and he was supposed to stop it with his feet. Now it took about fifteen boys to move the pipe so you can only imagine how large the pipes were. They rolled it and he put out his foot and the pipe rolled over it and crushed his foot and broke it. They carried him home and put him at the front door and ran and left him to face our parents all by himself. He was at the front door whimpering like a little puppy.

Who could punish a poor wounded, broken, crying child? Just say we should be the most obedient and well-directed people on earth because the rod of correction was our road map. Our parents didn't care anything about sparing the rod. We would go out to sing with the choir and man if we clowned around too much, Sister Pressley, the choir director, couldn't wait for us to get home. One night we stopped for ice cream after an engagement and all of us were just messing around. I guess we must have laughed too loud or something because we really didn't get in a whole lot of trouble. But Sister Pressley brought us home and walked us to the door. She told on us and then stood at the door to see what our parents would do. After a while, you heard screaming and hollering and saw a BIG smile on her face. Then the next day we were teased by all of the other children on the van because they heard us too. But then their parents said, "None of them could laugh because they got it too!"

We had a lot of engagements singing and going places with the choir and youth department. Sister Pressley had a van and she was faithful about picking us up and transporting us on a weekly basis. My fondest memories of my childhood were with Sister Pressley and the choir.

We were at the Osbys' home for a birthday party. The party was for one of the choir members so therefore, the entire choir was there. We had plenty of food and games and the boys just ran around having a good time. The girls just sat around talking as usual. The adults were inside, and one of them came out to bring more food and asked the boys to stop being so rough. Well that was like asking a hungry man who had not eaten in a week to deliver a pie across town. It just was not happening. They continued to run from each other playing "Tag" and "It." You see, back then we had very boring lives and it didn't take much to entertain us. We could take a milk carton and string and make a game and play for hours. We took brooms and braided them for hair; we took empty cola bottles and mops and made dolls; we took sheets and made tents; we took old car tires and hung them on a tree and made swings; we poured water on the sand and made mud and let it dry on our feet to make houses; we were inventors and didn't even know it at the time. But anyway, let's get back to the story. Marvin was a little younger than most of the other boys that were there. The boys were running around the house in circles and apparently they left him, so he decided that he would run in the opposite direction and catch up with them. Have you guessed it yet? He sure did! They did not see him coming and they all met around the corner, only to connect his head with one of the little boy's teeth. Everyone started screaming and crying, so when the parents came out they could not tell who was hurt. We all looked as if we were injured. Here we go again to the emergency room. Of course Marvin was dying if you let him tell it. He played the role until the very end. He could have won an Academy Award for his acting. He got home and we had to wait on him like live-in nurses or something. My parents had to pick him up and carry him, and Babro and I just stood by and looked and wanted to really cause bodily harm.

He was so pitiful! He had stitches and granted he had a large contusion on his head, but by this time that was normal. While he was mending, two of the missionaries from the church came by but our parents were not home. We were always told not to open the door for anybody while the parents were not home. But of course Babro said God would get us if we didn't open the door for the missionaries, so we did. They came in and anointed Marvin's bump on the head and prayed and prayed and prayed. So after they left, Babro wanted to get Marvin back so Babro told Marvin the missionaries had prayed for him and the bump on his head grew. Marvin got so scared and started crying.

Marvin wanted proof so Babro was supposed to go to my parents' room and get the hand mirror, but instead that nutcase brought back a magnifying glass and Marvin didn't know the difference. So the bump on his head did appear to be three times larger than what it was. He cried and cried until my parents got home, and when I told them what happened, Babro swore the bump REALLY grew. But you know after he said it so much, I'm not lying when I say the bump did appear to be growing. We thought we were getting Marvin back but we made it worse for ourselves. Since we made the bump grow (Mom said), we had to do all his chores and wait on him. This is over thirty years ago and Marvin is still trifling. He went to the Army as a parachutist, and I keep telling my parents and his wife that he was dropped on his head a time too many.

Mirror, Mirror, on My Knee

AS I SIT here and reflect, I remember one day while working and sitting in the company's car waiting for the public transportation bus to move from behind me, I felt this awful pain in my right knee. It happened so fast until I could not figure out right away what was going on. Then I looked at the knee and it was bleeding and swelling so rapidly. I saw the rearview mirror and it had fallen and the steel piece of the corner of the back of the mirror had stuck into my knee and I just sat there in disbelief. I eventually got out of the car and tried to walk, and to my surprise I could not. Or should I say to my not- so-surprise, because I had realized by now that anything that could go wrong would go wrong. It was like I had a magnet saying, "Trouble, come and find me!" I eventually had to have surgery to repair the knee. No one would believe a little mirror could do so much damage, but it certainly did.

Then years later, the mirror on my personal vehicle fell and did the same exact thing. I wondered how in the world could this happen not once but twice in a person's lifetime? And I (needless to say) have never heard of this happening to anyone else. While we are talking about incidents, there are a couple of more weird things that happened. One day I was in the store (and I will change the store name) Window Mart, just shopping when I saw some smart water bottles in the middle of the aisle. I went over to remove one and the entire display of water bottles fell and hit my foot. Stop acting as if you don't know what happened next. My foot started to throb and swell up so bad I could not walk on it, neither could I put back on my shoe. One of the associates in the food court gave me some ice to put on it and I had to buy a slipper to put on. No, I didn't sue, but now thinking of it, I should have gotten an attorney because I did have medical bills and pain and suffering. Well anyways it's over.

Girl Scout Leader

WHILE WORKING WITH the housing authority, I volunteered as a Girl Scout leader. Actually I was given the position, but it sounds a whole lot better to say I volunteered. So we went along during the year and we did have a pretty good group of little girls. It was a terrific troop. Not good enough to make me stay for the second term, but a good troop.

So we are at the end of the year, and some brilliant mind suggested camping—in the woods, in a tent, on a sleeping bag, with no hot running water. I guess you know by now, I am NO CAMPER. I do not like the outdoors at all! This had to be job security! So there were two other women with me. Diane was another leader who had no experience but took the challenge. We did have a leader who had been a leader for many years, so she was definitely in charge. We were supposed to leave earlier that day but things just kept popping up. It seemed as if we could not get a good start for nothing. I suggested it was a sign that we should not go, but do you think anyone listened?

It was very late. As a matter of fact it was close to sunset, but everyone (except me) was anxious to get going. We loaded up the van, got all the supplies and the girls, and headed to the campground. By the time we got there it was pitch-black and we could not see ANYTHING. So Natalie, who was supposed to know more than I did, decided that we would just camp where we were and find the correct site the following morning. We were given instructions, and the leaders assisted the girls who knew more than I did, Thank God. But we finally got the tents up after several hours. They told me how important it was to clear the area where you were lying so it would be a little more comfortable. I couldn't see where it made any difference. I just put the sleeping bag on the ground so I could get some rest.

Some Einstein suggested a walk in the woods to observe and I had two choices. Either I had to go with the group or stay in the woods by myself. So I decided to go along. It was fun finally, everyone singing and skipping and laughing, and it was a good feeling to see the girls enjoying themselves… when we heard this noise that sounded like a bear close to us. Before we could grab hold to the group, they were running and screaming and freaking out. Then we heard this voice saying, "I'm sorry, I didn't mean to frighten anyone. I was just joking around." It was the boyfriend of the head leader bringing the other supplies that could not be carried in the van. He was so apologetic, but then we hear a little voice saying "I think something is wrong with…," and then she points to one of the other girls. We looked and the little girl was holding her arm and it was swollen and we got nervous. By this time it is very late and the girls are exhausted, but we have to take her to the hospital. So Diane and I had to stay at the camp with the other girls while Natalie leaves us two in charge. Now remember, we are the two who knew absolutely NOTHING about camping. After several hours they returned and the little girl had on a cast. Her arm was broken when she fell and all of the other girls fell on top of her. Her parents were contacted, and they were very understanding. The girl was showing her cast and was getting all the attention from the other little girls. We finally got everyone calmed down and we decided (or should I say, I decided) that we should head back home the next morning.

At sunrise we heard noises outside the tent but no one was moving around because we were so tired from the night before. It had only been a few hours since we had gone to bed and the girls certainly were not moving around. So I continued to hear weird noises, so I yelled over to the next tent to Natalie for her to check things out. She went aside the tent, but leaned over and said, "Everyone just stay calm." Now you know the first thing a person does when they hear that is get nervous. We all peeped out and there were all kinds of animals surrounding us. They were eating because we did not realize the night before that we had parked and set up camp in the middle of the feeding ground. By that time a ranger was coming by and advised us to move camp. Well I informed him he was a tad-bit late, that we were on the same page as he was, and all he had to do was give us a few minutes and he would observe the fastest packing up he'd ever witnessed.

We got back home and delivered all the little girls and all they wanted to know was when the next trip would be. I could not figure out for the life of me why you would even considering going anywhere else with us, but they told their parents they had the best of time. I think the little girl with the broken arm's relatives took it quite well because she told them what a wonderful time she had. They were good people and members of my church at the time, and almost like family so they were very understanding and cooperative.

It's been over twenty-five years, and ask me how many more times have I been camping. You don't even have to ask because you already know the answer. It was an experience I never care to do again. I see some of the girls periodically and they are all doing quite well. I will ask them the next time I see them if any of them participated with the Girl Scouts with their own daughters.

No but seriously, every mother should experience this at least once. Why? I don't know, it just sounded like a good idea.

Neck Trouble

ONE NIGHT I had to run to K-Mart to pick up a few things. My husband asked if it could wait until the next day, and of course I said, "No it can't." So I get in the car and drive into the parking lot of K-Mart when I see headlights coming towards me. I turn to the left and the lights follow me. I turn to the right and they follow me coming head on to meet me. Then there was this awful bang and my head and neck seemed to go in different directions. I could not move and I was scared out of my wits because I had never experienced anything like this before. The man got out of the truck stumbling drunk, smelling like alcohol. He looked at me and tried to leave but there were two witnesses who ran to the truck and took the keys. He did not like this too well. The police department was called and I still was in the van with pain radiating down my neck and arms. I had my phone in my hands trying to make up in my mind if I was going to call my husband because we all know the rest of the story. So I decided to call him because I was going to have to be transported to the hospital. The officer was not very kind and/or helpful.

He took the information and I did not see him administer any test to the other driver or anything. It was around the time he was getting off from work, and it was very apparent he was not interested in making an arrest, because believe it or not, he LET THE DRIVER Leave! My husband goes on to say, "I'm not going to tell you right now 'I told you so,' but we will have a little talk later." I don't know what was worse, the pain in my neck, or knowing I had to hear a sermon from him.

It was determined that I had to have a cervical fusion and surgery was scheduled. I did get a copy of the police report and the officer never mentioned that the driver had been drinking or anything. I had a tag number from the truck and it was not registered, no insurance, and his name was Julio Gonzalez. Well that made my chances of finding him real easy, huh? Yeah right! There were at least 300 of them in the city and no way of finding the driver because the officer let him go. I did make a complaint to the police department and got nowhere, and I started to take it to the next level, but then I started having terrible nightmares about officers coming to my home and killing me and all kinds of crazy things were going on in my head. So I did drop it and realized how stupid I really was. Because now here I am ready for surgery, and even though the insurance will pay 80% of the bills, I was stuck with the 20%, and needless to say, it was very expensive. That was 1998, and now this is 2011 and three surgeries later and over $200,000.00 of medical bills and still not compensated. I have two metal plates and six screws in my neck and knee, and if anyone wants to know what the weather is going to be like for the day, just call. During this ordeal I developed RSD, a crippling disease, and for years I could not walk. It was said that within 10 years I would be totally confined to a wheelchair, but thanks to God Almighty, I am walking. Still have neck pain, and as a matter of fact, as I write this book, I am scheduled for surgery in about four weeks. I only wish I had not let my fears get the best of me. It's called watching too much TV. You see how officers come and kill witnesses and how the police department is corrupt on TV, so you begin to exaggerate, but seriously in many instances they go unreported for the same fear.

Well so much for that. I considered myself a pretty decent and kind person and often wondered how my life would have turned out if I had not taken the path I did. You always look at others who blatantly live their lives as if God doesn't exist, and they appear to prosper and be in good health. OK I know I'm not having a pity party because I know what the scriptures say about those who put their trust in God. Through that entire ordeal, I found out that if you take care of God's business, He surely will take care of yours.

Now you see how I ended the statement above, right? That's where I stopped last night on my way to church for prayer meeting. I got to church and I saw that someone was renting our church for the night, so I followed some of the members of my church to the fellowship hall. I met the head elder and some of the members, and it was decided that service would be in the fellowship hall for the night. We began singing and having a good time, and the music was just divine. No piano, no organ, and no drums, just clapping and singing from the depth of our souls. Then the Bible study elder assigned for the lesson came forth from the book of Daniel and encouraged us in that we will reap if we faint not. We were at the end of the service and asked to stand for prayer. We all stood up and after prayer I began to sit, when I HIT THE FLOOR! Somehow the chair had moved from under me and I had nowhere to go but down, and did I ever. Folk started to run over to assist me (those that were not laughing of course), and it was a sight to see. One of the young men said to me afterwards that it appeared that I was falling in slow motion. But come to think of it, it was like I was just floating for awhile until I hit that cold, hard ceramic tile. I saw people snickering and trying not to let me see them laugh, but I couldn't even get mad because I know if I had seen what they had just witnessed, I would have gotten a little chuckle in myself. The long story short, one of the sisters said, "Make sure you go home and soak in some Epsom salt because you are going to be very sore in the morning." Let me tell you that it did not help! By the time I got home it was like a freight train had hit me and backed up and ran over me again. My neck, back, and legs were in pain, and all I could think about was how ashamed I was. I am writing this the very next night and I'm still stiff and sore, but with pain medication and the love and support of family members (all except from Cassandra, my sister-in-law), it will be OK. I'm able to write just this little portion tonight. I've had a long night and day and I need a little rest so I will pick this up in a day or so. Please pray that I will be able to continue writing about past experiences and no additional new ones.

It's already hard to keep up with the hundreds of things that previously happened to me.

22nd Surgery/Procedure

IT HAS BEEN about three months since the last entry of this book. You guessed it right. I have been in the hospital for my 22nd surgery. This was a very hard surgery. I had three previous cervical fusions of the spine and the surgeon previously cut the front of my neck, but this time he had to go through the back of the neck. The surgery was supposed to have been about two and a half hours, but it went almost six hours. I was told I had complications during surgery and had to have a blood transfusion. It is a habit for me to inquire about the time when coming out of surgery to thank God for allowing me to come out all right! But out of all the surgeries, I cannot remember ever coming out of this surgery until the next day. That had never happened before. Well I guess I did OK or I would not be sitting here telling you about it. I have been home recuperating slowly but surely.

The first two weeks home from the hospital were so painful and unbearable. I could not find a comfortable position for anything. I literally had to go to the restroom and/or shower and back to the couch. My bed was too high for me to climb in so I had to bunk out on the couch. Weeks have gone by and I'm up and moving about. I just have to keep reminding myself that I'm not completely healed yet and not to overdo it. I was hoarse due to the fact that the doctor had to put this metal plate and screws so close to the vocal cord. I was told that I may never sing again because of the hardware in my neck and the scar tissue that had been formed. But I am glad to say God has allowed me to keep a reasonable portion of my voice to sing praises to Him.

I had so many family members, friends, and church members to come by and offer support and food. It was truly a blessing to see how everyone poured so much love into my family when we needed it the most. The elders of the church came by and offered prayer, which was so rewarding due to the fact that I could not attend church.

Physical therapy is very challenging, and I also have acupuncture, which is going quite well. My voice is fragile and I'm hoarse a lot; my neck is restricted in range of motion; stiffness and pain every time it rains; I have a high sensitivity to hot or cold; I cannot lift anything over 10 pounds; sometimes I can't move at all and I have to wait for hours before I'm mobile, but there is a song that says, "I don't feel no ways tired, because I don't believe God would bring me this far to leave me."

Let me seeeee. There is something else I wanted to share about this surgery but I cannot for the life of me remember what it was. Maybe I will think about it later on in the book and I promise to let you know. It was vital to my recovery, but why can't I remember what it is? Oh well, let's move on. Oh it was......... no, that's not it either! We'll come back to it after I remember it.

Fire in the Hotel

ONE NIGHT MY husband had to work late and then early the next morning, so he decided that we would spend the night at a hotel in Melbourne where he works. The girls and I watched TV until it got very late and then we finally fell asleep, only to be awakened around midnight by the fire alarm.

We heard people running and screaming, so I got the girls up and we heard the intercom instructing us to head for the stairs so we did. I had my two little girls (and by the way, I was already on crutches already) running and Zylandria was running so fast she got ahead of us. I was terrified because someone opened the door to another floor and hit my knee as hard as a hammer and I went to the floor. I lost view of her and didn't know if she had been run over by the crowd or what. We finally got outside and she ran over to me and everyone was crying and tense and sleepy. I looked around and there was smoke in the building and we were informed that it would be awhile before we could go back in. I felt my knee aching but did not notice right away that it was bleeding so badly until my shoe was squishing from the blood. I had my cell phone and called Willis, and he did not seem to be surprised at all that something had gone wrong. He said this was only one of the number of things that could go wrong as usual. I wanted to get mad but what the heck; he was right. Something was always happening as you can see. I was transported to the hospital and treated and released, and do you know the hotel tried to make us pay for the stupid room after I almost lost my life and leg and children. Well that's a little dramatic, but you get the picture, it could have happened that way. Do a survey! How many think I should have paid for the room, raise your hand? Did you really raise your hand? You are as messed up in the head as I am. Well needless to say I never spent another night at this establishment. Good riddance.

Lady with the $100 Bill

I **WAS YOUNG** and still living at home with my parents, when one late evening we were just sitting around talking and we heard neighbors arguing. Well it's not as if we had never heard this before because the old man would drink every weekend and he always wanted to argue and fight with his wife. So we grew accustomed to hearing this on a regular basis. But for some reason he was extra loud this evening. We heard his wife saying, "G'on, Jake, leave me alone; I ain't got your money." He said, "You got my $100 bill and I may be drunk but I ain't that drunk!" This went on for about an hour. Then the noise got closer to our backyard and it was hard to ignore. She kept telling him she did not have his money, that he must have gotten drunk and lost it. She said she did not have his $100 bill, but he insisted that she did. My mom said, "Why doesn't he let that woman alone! Can't he see she does not have his money?" The woman kept getting closer and closer to the house because I think she wanted my parents to come out and say something, but we just thought they were having their usual romantic drunk-on-fight for the weekend. Things began to quiet down and we saw him walk down the street away from the house. About two hours later we heard our doorbell ring and the wife was at the door. She said, "Pastor Ingram, does anyone have change for a $100 bill?" My mom said, "Well sir! I never in a million years would have believed the woman had actually taken the man's money," and we laughed so hard and the wife said, "Well he was so drunk, someone was going to take it and it might as well have been me."

About twenty-five years later, the church was having a yard sale for our feeding program and pantry and that same lady came up and asked the pastor if we had change for $100. We had a big laugh about it. Some things never get old!!

Who Is That Person?

ONE LATE AFTERNOON my dad was sitting in the kitchen eating shrimp fried rice. I had never had any allergies and/or reactions to shellfish.

However, recently I had some itching and some reactions so I had stopped eating shellfish. Chinese fried rice is a favorite and it looked so good, so I had my dad give me a spoonful of the rice without the shrimp. I figured if I just had the rice it would be OK. WRONG! I started to itch and feel funny so my mom suggested Benadryl. I said I had some at home so I left to go home to get some. By the time I got halfway home my girls were looking at me strangely so I looked in the rearview mirror and what did I see? I was unrecognizable and my throat was closing up and I couldn't breathe. I was minutes from the hospital so I telephoned my parents to come to the hospital for the girls and for them to contact Willis at work.

I heard my dad when he got to the emergency room asking for me and they told him where I was but when he looked in, he didn't recognize me and told the nurse she had given him the wrong room number and that could not be his child. Well it was and he actually could not recognize me because at this point I was looking like the Incredible Hulk. They began to treat me and gave me injections of steroids and God only knows what else, but within the hour I was feeling and looking like myself. By that time Willis had made it there and was looking at me and I could tell by his facial expression that I still looked horrible. He kept asking questions and I was trying not to tell him what had happened. The nurse knew and she said something like I had a bad reaction and it was not determined what the cause was. I learned a valuable lesson that day. Even though I did not eat the shrimp, apparently enough of the shrimp was in the rice. We always try to appease our appetites and think we have all the answers, but something always goes wrong when we don't abide and do the right thing. I could have avoided upsetting family members and another doctor bill by doing the right thing!!!

One night I slipped going into the shower, but this should not count against me because my darling husband's shampoo wasted in the shower and I did not see it. As soon as I walked in I hit the shower wall with my mouth and I just knew I didn't have any teeth left in my mouth. This was the most pain I had experienced in a long time. My mouth was bleeding and I was terrified to look in the mirror. I didn't have any ice at home so I sent my niece and daughter down to my parents' home to get some. I thought I was going to need stitches but I did not go to the hospital because by this time, I was really sick and tired of the hospital. Several years later there is still a scar on my lip, but thank God I did not lose any teeth. One tooth was kind of shaky for awhile but it finally got all right.

New York Experience

YOU THOUGHT THAT was pitiful, just listen to this. A few years ago I traveled to New York for a funeral of a son of a good friend of mine. I'm going to just call her Jackie. Well, she is a very special friend so of course I had to be there for her. We flew from Florida to New York and it was cold because it was in January, but no snow yet. I had never seen snow before and I was hoping to do so before we headed back to Florida.

This was a very (how can I say it?) interesting visit. On our way from the funeral to the repast, two of Jackie's sisters decided to have a heated discussion on the busiest interstate road in New York. There is SO MUCH MORE that happened in the car but due to the fact that the story is about my experience and not theirs, I will leave it for another book. Well a small portion of what happened is the oldest sister was in the backseat of the younger sister's car. The oldest sister would not shut up for anything in the world and she got on the younger sister's nerves, so the younger sister decided that it was her car and she was going to put her out on the interstate. She opened the door and the older sister was holding on to the seat of the car for dear life and she was just kicking and they were pulling and kicking like crazy, and all you had to do at this point was get a bag of popcorn because it was like looking at a reality show at the movie theater.

The oldest sister's daughter said, "Auntie, just go on!" Then she turned to her mother and said, "Mommy, shut up or I swear to God I will stab you with these scissors in my purse." Of course the older sister didn't shut up but we were back on the road again, and I just shook my head in disbelief. If that was just a little bit of the story I could share, then use your imagination to figure out the rest of the ride.

So after the repast we headed back to the house and I was getting my purse out of the trunk of the car when I felt a bump on my backside and then the trunk fell down on my hand. Oh boy is right! It slammed down on my hand and started to throb. I looked and it was two of Jackie's church members coming over to visit. I think he just wanted to scare me a little or was just playing, but little did he know he was dealing with the Queen of Accidents and if it could happen, it certainly would happen. I went in and my hand started to throb, but I didn't want to make it obvious because I didn't want to offend anyone. I lay on the couch and we talked and I ate a little something, and then it was time to go back over to where I was staying. Around 5:00 am I went into the living room and Jackie heard me and came out and my hand was as large as an elephant's hand. I told her I felt bad for having to wake her up after just burying her son, but I had been in pain all night and I could not stand it any longer. So now I'm in the hospital in New York. They put a cast on it and told me to follow up with my doctor when I got back home. I was hesitating calling my husband because I knew what he was going to say. And he did! Can I send you anywhere and you not come back banged up? But seriously look at it, again this was not my fault this time. The next night before we were leaving to go back to Florida, it did snow and it was beautiful. My first snow experience and you already know I fell and almost killed myself sliding under the car. Jackie tried to give me lessons on how to walk in the snow, but I didn't need them because I decided for all purposes I would stay in until time to go. Since I was there for a funeral I asked what do they do with the bodies if there is so much snow on the ground, and she said she had never thought of that in all the years she had lived in New York. Go figure! Considering I do not like the cold, it was a delight to be back at home.

If It Could Go Wrong, It Did!

I **WAS IN** the hospital after having a hysterectomy. I was told to move around so I wouldn't get gas. Earlier in this hospital stay I had a problem with my veins and they had to disconnect me from the IV. It was disconnected for almost a day and standing in the corner when a nurse came in and asked me why was I not connected. I thought it was a riddle because she is the nurse and she is asking the patient why they are not connected. She looked at the charts and said she was connecting me immediately. She pulled the pole out of the corner and connected the IV again. Then I had to go to the restroom and got up and tried to walk with the pole when the wheels came from under it and I hit the side of the bed and fell over. I screamed so loud until the nurse came running in to assist. I told her that the wheels of the pole tilted some kind of way and I fell and burst a few of the stitches. She patched me up and left as if nothing had happened. That was a HORRIBLE hospital stay but what can you say, it is what it is.

After so many visits to the hospital, my husband swears the hospital knows us by name. He says there is a special wing reserved just for me because they expect something to go wrong and they are waiting. It does seem to appear to be so. But I'm looking forward to the day when I'm accident free. I remember when I was at the Lifestyle Center, they took blood work and sent me to a specialist because they suspected leukemia. With my history the first thought was it could be true. But then I began to pray and ask God to show Himself Great and Mighty in my life. I had been really battling with incidents, injuries, emergencies, sickness, and

I was really tired of the enemy raging havoc in my life. After extensive tests and so forth, whatever they thought they saw was no longer there. But I forgot to tell you about the first night and first time at the Lifestyle Center. The Lifestyle Center is a holistic clinic where you are treated with natural home remedies and natural medication and teas. There are many treatments using water, heat, and ice.

But my very first visitation to the center, that morning around 5:30 am there was a knock on the door. I forgot to tell you it is pitch-dark because there are no street lights and you are in the country surrounded by mountains and there is complete silence and darkness. Well, the knock on the door startled me so badly until I rolled off of this little small twin bed and hit the floor so hard.

The counselor came in and turned on the light, but by this time I was saying "In Jesus name, Amen" as if I had been on my knees praying. It took all she had not to laugh because I know she realized what had really happened. She asked if she could assist me in any way and I reassured her I was all right, so she said I only had a few minutes to get to the lab so I quickly got up off my knees, but not before thanking God for not allowing me to break my neck.

I started to think about some of the good things that happened. I thought about one day when I was much younger how I remember seeing an angel and how I have that image in my head many, many years later. I also remember how one night I dreamed about this little old lady that Ma-Maggie used to be a live-in caretaker for. Ma-Maggie is like a second mom. She is actually the mother of my sister-in-law. If you want lessons on how to pinch someone or hug someone, she is the one to come to. She can pinch and hugs like a bear! I saw the little lady in my dream on Juanita Avenue around the curve the night before.

Ma-Maggie called and said the little lady climbed in a chair and unlatched the door. The latch was placed high so she could not open the door, but somehow she did and left the house walking.

I got in my car and drove over to where I had seen her in my dream, and lo and behold she was standing there. It took me a minute to get my thoughts together to figure out what had happened. Many times I would dream and it would come to pass. I often wondered if I dreamed the winning lotto number if I would play! I have never played, but I did dream that some couple won some millions of dollars and said they remembered me and how I had helped them many years ago and they wanted to give me a donation for my programs because they knew I would continue to help people. Well I will! (smile) Just feel free to send it and I will continue to help. You see, years ago I actually was a social worker, and I remember working for the housing authority and helping two families buy beds because the children didn't have anything to sleep on. I also remember when one of the clients' daughters ran into a hot water tank with her motor bike and it exploded and she had to be airlifted to the hospital. The mother could not ride with the airplane so I rented her a car and gave her gas money. The list goes on and on, and to tell you the truth if everyone who borrowed money from me (not the ones I gave money but loaned it) paid me back, I probably would be sitting pretty good right now. We have a feeding program where we feed thousands each month, and not one week has gone by where we didn't have at least bread and fruit for them to eat. This is a volunteer program with no funding other than donations. So much for that!

I was in college and someone told me this couple was looking for a babysitter at night for about three to four nights a week. She said the pay was good and I thought I would give it a try. So I met the couple and they appeared to be okay so I said I would take the job. Well it was about a month or so and the job was easy, just getting there around 9:30 pm or 10:00 pm each night and for the most part, the baby would be sleeping. The parents worked out of the home so I had time to study and do homework. Then I noticed little strange things. He started to beat the wife and I would hear her crying, and then a few nights she came in where the baby and I were for safety because I guess she felt he would not hit her in front of me. That was a little nerve-wracking and I began to feel uncomfortable. I prayed about it and to tell the truth, I didn't want to give it up because I can't remember what the pay was but I do remember it was good for what I had to do. But that last night did it for me. They would come home around 6:00 am each morning and then he hit her and she was crying. The things he was saying were making me think she was a prostitute, and I got so nervous but I didn't want to show it so I played it off. But I was saying to myself, PJ, when you get out of here, don't ever come back. There was a little overnight case I kept there but I didn't care. I left it because I did not want them to know I suspected anything and that I was never going back. Talking about naïve! I didn't have a clue. That's what your parents mean when they say God looks after babies and fools. Don't know which one I was, but all I do know is He protected me from seen and unseen dangers.

It was early one morning and I was sitting in the repair shop waiting for my car when I noticed a gentleman stumbling out of the restroom with his shirt unbuttoned and his tie was crooked. He was walking like he was drunk and everyone just stood there watching. I finally got up and walked around the corner and observed some of the other employees trying to assist him. I got closer and had prayer with him and asked God to be with him because he was in bad shape. This was around 9:00 am on the south side of the county. Then again around 2:30 pm, my daughter Dominique had an appointment and we got to CMS early so she asked if we could go to the store for a snack before her appointment. We were close to a Circle K so I thought we had time to go over and come back in time for her appointment. Not having this planned, we ran into the Circle K only to find a woman standing at the soda machine just crying and all upset.

So I spoke and asked if she was okay, and wouldn't you know it she began to try to explain to me, and by this time I'm saying to myself, doesn't she know I really didn't mean for her to talk to me? I was only asking out of courtesy but I was sure that was the end of it. She went on and on to explain how her husband was in the hospital and how he got sick at work at a car dealer's this morning and he has to have emergency surgery. This is the same man from this morning. Did you notice the time difference from this morning and this afternoon? Five and a half hours later I ran into the woman of the husband I had just had prayer with. There is no way our paths should have met, only that God had arranged it that way. Do you know how many places I had been since that morning? I immediately joined hands with her and Dominique and offered prayer and assured her that he would be all right. I explained to Dominique what had happened and she just looked at me as if to say, "AND?"

God wanted me to sit down and think about my life and how the good does outweigh the bad. I was having a pity party about how things were happening. But God reminded me of Peter in the boat in Matthew 14:32. As long as Peter's eyes were on Jesus he was able to walk on water. It was only when he looked down and took his eyes off Jesus that he began to sink. We too can walk on the waters of our situations and be able to withstand without sinking.

I am convinced that everyone's got a story and I will not throw in the towel; I will not waste the pain and agony, NEITHER proclaim defeat. Satan peeped into my future and saw what God was doing in my life and about to do and he didn't like it at all. But I'm reassured that God knows what we don't know. He sees what we can't see. I almost let go but I'm persuaded nothing or No one will separate me from the Love of God. I had to learn to resist the urge to settle and you can too. God has a way of taking His little lambs, wandering sheep, lying on their backs and picking them up and placing them on their feet again. David said in the scriptures so profoundly that we must encourage ourselves, because there is more to life than what's happening that moment.

Real Joy, Peace, and Happiness is knowing the best is yet to come. The whole ordeal of each of our lives can be used as a strengthening tool if you allow it to. Ask yourself the question, Am I a blessing to anyone or anything? Will I be missed if I die? Did my life make a difference to someone who was in need or did I just exist? Did I accomplish any of my obtainable goals and/or expectations? Will my family be proud to say that I'm a vital asset to the family rather than a liability? Am I a part of the answer to a situation, or am I the problem?

I would have liked to share more of my life with you, but my parents may have had a fool for a child, but it wasn't me. Don't think I'm just going to put everything in here just to sell a book. No, but on the serious side, just wanted to share a little about myself and some experiences to encourage someone who is going through trial after trial in their own life. There is sunshine after the rain. I too was sinking deep in sin, far from the peaceful shore, but His Love, Jesus' love, lifted me; now safe am I. My prayer is that for each individual who reads this book, their life will be touched and receive the blessing they stand in the need of. I almost threw in the towel, but I simply allowed Him to brush me off where I had fallen, and stand me back up on higher ground. When I allowed Him to lead, it was like a flash of light in my life and I was able to see, where at one time there was utter darkness. Reach out and touch the hem of His garment. His touch has tremendous power over any storm, situation, mountain, valley, or demon. How can you remain calm when the whole world seems like it has turned against you? I felt the pressure was being a PK and always being under the spotlight, having to remain immaculate. But the genuine fact is that Satan comes to kill, steal, and destroy, and he does not fight fair.

As I reflect on the story of the leper in the Bible, I'm reminded of how he made his way to Jesus even after being instructed not to enter the city. He made the conscious decision to go regardless of the consequences. He had one thing in his favor: no one wanted to touch him to put him out of the city because they were afraid of getting the dreadful disease. He did not care because he knew Christ could make him whole. I could hear him singing the song, "What can wash away my sins, nothing but the blood of Jesus. What can make me whole again, nothing but the blood of Jesus."

There was a story of a son who went off to war but he loved his mother very much. He was across seas for many years on a special mission. The story goes on to say that one day the man died and his best friend came to bring some of his belongings to the mother for his dear friend. The friend was startled to scrutinize the atrocious living conditions of the home. The mother went on to say she was barely making it, and at one point she didn't know where her next meal was coming from. The soldier was dumbfounded because he knew for a fact his friend sent money home to her every month.

So he asked her if she got the money each month and she said no, but she said she was not worried because as long as her son was doing well, then so was she. She went on to say the only thing he sent me each month was these beautiful pictures and postcards. The soldier looked around the room in utter disbelief as he saw every wall of her bedroom covered with savings bonds and money. She did not realize he was sending her money for years and thus, she lived in poverty and shame. A lot of us are just like that old lady. We have gifts, talents, and ambitions, but we are ignorant, not being aware of what we have.

There is nothing like a good test to keep you on your knees, but let us not get weary in well doing for we shall reap if we faint not.

As I reflected on part of my life, having once the desire to end it all, the question and focus remains the same. Am I spiritually enriched or am I going to give up? The answer is, I have decided to make Jesus my choice.

Do you remember earlier in the book when I said I had something to share with you but I forgot it, but when I remembered that I would let you know? Well last night I remembered it and I laughed so hard. I said to myself, Self, get up and make a note in case you forget it again. Then I just lay there because I just knew I would not forget this. It was too good to forget. You guessed it, I forgot it again and I'm soooooooo mad because I wanted to share this moment with the readers.

But I did remember how one day my brothers and I and some of our friends were riding our horse my dad bought us. They seemed to be having a good time, and I was afraid of the horse at first but then as time went by I got used to him. We were taking turns riding but Babro, as I told you earlier, always had to step it up a notch. He wanted to ride and ride and not give anyone else a chance. So it was my time to ride and he was mad because my dad made him get off and let me ride. I should have known he was up to no good because he helped me up on the horse, asked me if I was doing okay, reassured me of his support, and you would think a bell would have gone off in my head. So I went trotting along, and all of a sudden he takes a paddle and hits the horse so hard, and the horse takes off so fast and I fall off, but he had put my foot in the saddle in a way that I didn't just fall off. No, I was hanging off of the horse and the horse was dragging me down the road.

They were just running behind me trying to stop the horse and I was screaming and crying so loudly, my dad came running. They finally got the horse stopped, but when he stopped, I jerked and the horse stepped on my side and yes, it was very painful. I really took advantage of the situation.

Babro had to do all my chores for me. He was mad but I really made him pay dearly. Even though the horse stepped on my side, I had my arm bandaged and got some crutches, and I looked like I had been hit by a freight train.

Every time he passed by me I would smile, and he would get mad and tell my parents nothing was wrong with me. He got so mad when my parents would holler at him and make him leave me alone. I'll teach him to mess with me.

God has really been good to me. After all the things I went through, I have to acknowledge the fact that He has been a present help in time of trouble. I often think of the poem about footprints in the sand. It's so true, God is there carrying us even though we can't see Him. One day I was having a really bad day. There are times things are going on and you can't even talk to family or friends about them. I asked God one day to show Himself to me, and that I wanted to see His hand of Mercy in my life. I kid you not! Zee came home with this little hand she drew at school and it had written on it the scripture Philippians 4:19: "My God will supply all your needs." There's a song that says, "He may not come when you want Him to, but He's an on-time God, yes He is." That song says it all. He's such a God that He often comes when we need Him to.

I again would like to take this opportunity to thank my family for being so supportive in my time of illness, sickness, distress, depression, anxiety, and withdrawal from medication. I spent a lot of time in the hospital and back and forth to doctor appointments, physical therapy, MRI's. X-rays, CAT scans, and so forth. But I could not have asked for a better family in regards to a strong support system. My parents traveled back and forth to help take care of me. They gave me an astronomical amount of hours, and if I had a million dollars I could not pay them back for being there for me. My in-laws, family, and friends were there for me every step of the way. But my supreme support system was my immediate family, Willis and my two girls. For over fifteen years I have been sick, and at one point in my life I could not walk and was so swollen all the time. They took care of me, and you can tell just how much people love you when you get sick and cannot do for yourself. We learned how to love each other and take care of each other through our turmoil.

All of us had a little issue here and there. Dominique was born with a hole in her heart and asthma. Before she turned eighteen months, she had three surgeries. ZeeZee just had her fourth surgery on her right foot, and she still continues to have major problems with it. Willis had a couple of kidney stones and you would think he was in labor or something. But we all were there for each other. There were times when I was on several medications, even to the point where I had to give myself injections. The pain would get so severe until sometimes the medication seemed to stop working. But on several occasions, Willis would pray and just being near him, the warmth from his body would ease the pain.

I kid you not, there were times I would be sick all day, and as soon as he was getting off of work to come home, I would feel better. Now don't get me wrong, sometimes being near him did just the opposite. Just kidding, boo!

The doctor told me that at the end of the tenth year of my disease (RSD), I would probably be confined to a wheelchair, but it has been over eleven years and I am nowhere near being in a wheelchair.

As a matter of fact, a few weeks ago I was driving to the Circle K, feeling really good, thinking on the goodness of Jesus, smiling riding in my new car my husband bought me. I saw some guys looking my way, smiling and talking, and I could tell they were talking about me. So I got out of the car to go into the store, and they were pointing and talking louder and smiling with delight. So of course being the female I am, I nodded and they were saying, "Boy, does that look good. Uhmmmmm!!" I really started to strut and walk proudly. Then they asked (while looking now at the car), "What is the name of your car? What kind of car is that?" Talking about shame! Shame is not the word.

I could have gone through the floor, but you know I had to play it off as if I knew they were talking about the car. I hurried in and out of the store so I could get back in the car to laugh at myself.

There have only been a few times when I was so embarrassed. I remember the time when my friend Dana and I almost went to jail while we were out trying to play detective in the middle of the night. Can't give you the details but it was Fuuunny. We called ourselves going to catch someone and we got caught for trespassing, and the funny thing is we had the wrong house, wrong person, and wrong motorcycle. And I would tell you about the night I dropped Dana over to her friend's house and the house was dark and we thought he was having a candlelight dinner. Come to find out, his lights were off. But I'm not going to tell you about it unless she gives me permission to do so, so stop asking because I'm not telling.

So you ask the question(s), "How do I get there? How do I make the connection to God? How do I strip away the anger? P.J., you talked to me in this book about your experiences and how you made it, but how can I do the same?"

Well, let me see if I can help you. A story comes to mind about a baby elephant that was in a circus, and since he was a baby and so small they tied his feet to a small pole and he could not get away. He didn't have the strength at that time so he struggled daily with it and somehow figured he just could not get away so he became contented with the idea of being there. He was in the circus for many years and they continued to tie his feet on the pole and he remained there, and one day the question was asked as to why the elephant wouldn't move. Well it was determined that he had accepted the fact that he could not get away for so long until it became a part of life to him. He accepted defeat, and even though he had grown and become stronger, his mind was telling him he could not do it. That's how Satan is with us. He is like a roaring lion and he has scared us into thinking we have gone so far, done so much, sunk so low until God cannot forgive us. Ephesians tells us that there is no length, height, depth, or width to God's love. First we have to acknowledge the fact that we will have our battles or weapons or Isaiah 54:17 would not have said we would. But the scripture does not stop there. It reinforces the fact that the weapon formed against us will not prosper.

My prayer began to be each morning "God, here I am. I want you to order my footsteps, guide me, handle this day, and give me a blueprint of how you think things should go today."

I had to go into my secret place and share my hurts that I could not (dared not) share with anyone else. I was taught early in life not to question God, but in all honesty I thought He owed me something. I felt that I had a monopoly on God and He should be doing better by me. I was the pastor's daughter supporting the ministry, being the good PK, and this is all I'm getting out of life? Of course, He certainly had me mistaken for someone else. Until one day I was sitting in the office of the church and He had me put on a blindfold over my eyes and asked me, "What can you see?" I could not see anything and He had me just sit there in the darkness for a while, and I started to cry because it was dark and I was alone and I did not like it but I knew there was a lesson in it for me. Then He had me take the blindfold off and explained to me that in the midst of all my trials and tribulations, it seemed as if I was in a dark place, a hole and appeared to be alone, but He was my eyes, ears, hands, and feet while I was in a dark place. I did not, could not, see Him because Satan had me believing I was all alone, but God let me know that He directed my paths just as I had asked Him to do. He was a present help and even though He did not come when I thought He should, He was ALWAYS on time. I continued to try to see Him during my storms; even though the way was cloudy, I continued to look towards the hill from where my help comes from.

But seriously, God has shown himself to be whatever I have needed Him to be. He's been a provider, shelter, food and clothing, a healer, counselor, protection, friend, guidance, way maker, and my all-and-all. He can and will be the same for you, because He has no favorites; He does not love me any more than He loves you.

My husband and I prayed and decided to focus on a different kind of ministry. We started to pick out a young person one at a time and mentor them, having prayer with them twice a day until they got on track. Then we went on to the next young person and we found out that as long as we were helping and encouraging someone else, we did not have the time to waste focusing on ourselves. There is an old saying that if everyone put their problems in a sack and reached in and got someone else's problem, we would be scrambling trying to get our little problem back.

How do you get there? Psalms 91:1-16 encourages me knowing that God gave His angels charge over me and that all I have to do is call and He will answer. He is an awesome God and I found out just how He loved me. There are some things, friends, relationships, and situations we need to get out of, but we are too stubborn and selfish until God just has to do what He does best, and that is sometimes allowing us to go through things to get our attention. My life has been a testimony to so many because just to look at me, you cannot tell the amount of metal plates and screws in my body; you can't see the RSD in my body; you can't see the severe pain, and yet my testimony is "God is Good" in spite of. Look at the word "testimony" and see what the prefix is. Yes, TEST!

There is no testimony without a test. Just like the elephant we are holding on to stuff, guilt, pain, and the list goes on and on, but it's time to let it go, forgive yourself, and allow God to make you complete that only comes through Him.

1 Peter 5:7 says, "Cast all (not some) of your cares on Him because He does care for you." There is no river long enough, no mountain high enough, no valley too deep that He cannot save. He specializes and can do what no other power can do. How can you overcome? I can only share with you how I did it, but you have to search yourself and find that secret place and ask for your own blueprint for your life. But let me tell you this one thing: God does not love me any more than He loves you, nor does He love you any more than He loves me or anyone else. He is just and loving and faithful and I just Thank Him for not giving me what I deserved but instead He had mercy me. Fear is the greatest weapon Satan uses to keep us in bondage. Through these situations I found coping skills and it's called P-R-A-Y-E-R. In all things continue "Thanksgiving." With so many scars, metal, and screws in my body it causes a sense of loss, grief, a change that is hard to cope with, but I found comfort, healing, and insight through it all knowing that All things do work together for our good according to His plan.

But keep this one thing in mind: make sure you mean what you say when you ask God for an assignment. I prayed one morning for an opportunity to be a witness for Him. So I forgot about it as the day went on. My sister Donna and I were walking over the bridge as a part of our exercise regimen. We had walked over the bridge to one side and we were headed back when we noticed a man standing on the other side of the bridge as if something was wrong. He was pacing back and forth and then he walked and stepped up on the bridge as if he was going to jump. Donna said we need to do something, and I said you are right, I'm running the opposite way. I reminded her how when a person is drowning and you try to save them, sometimes they will grab you and you drown and they live. She started to cross the bridge but there was traffic coming, but she wanted to say something to him.

By this time the man steps up high and we begin to yell at him. I'm yelling of course as I RUN the other way, and then he jumps and I scream and I grab my cell phone and dial 911 and inform them of what was going on. I didn't stop until I got to the other side. I looked down and my knuckles were bleeding from where I hit them on the brick wall; my watch was broken with the hands and spring dangling out of it; my hair was flying in every direction; I had lost one of my contacts; I had a hazel eye and a brown eye looking real crazy; my clothes halfway on and one shoe on. By this time I see Donna coming on the bridge and then the police were arriving and I was asking her questions and she laughed and shook her head at me. We saw Channel 12 News on the bridge and they wanted to talk to someone who had witnessed the incident. Two teenage boys came along and pretended to have seen everything, but I did not care because I was not getting on national television looking like a crazy woman. I was bleeding and limping so badly until I'm surprised they didn't think I had tried to jump. Then it came to me just as clear as crystal the very thing I had asked (to be used that day) to witness and help someone, that I almost killed myself running from the opportunity. Each day we all can do something to make someone else's day a little brighter.

There are times when you will want to take your life or pack your things and just leave and start all over again. I have vowed to always have encouraging words for everyone I meet. Anyone who knows me will tell you that each time you ask me how I'm doing, my reply is "All is well, I have no complaints."

If you take nothing else from this book, just remember to be encouraged, knowing that the best is most definitely still yet to come!

I Almost Gave Up, but Giving Up Is Not an Option Anymore!
BE BLESSED.

About the Author and the Purpose of his book

IT WAS FASCINATING to think how my life appeared so well put together by so many other people, but deep down inside I knew the threads were coming apart at the seams. Several events and/or experiences of years past and present brought this notion to mind to share with family, friends, and readers the tremendous blessings of endurance.

It is especially important to focus on the fact that you can be a preacher's kid and grow up all your life in church and still find yourself in a dark place of no return.

This book has been written primarily for the person who is hurting whom the enemy has told there is no way out. It is critical for you to be aware that it is OK to feel out of touch at times, but also to know you don't have to face your fears alone.

There were scriptures and stories used in this book for demonstration from the King James Version of the Bible.

This book comes from the depth of my heart, knowing now that we can survive our trials and tribulations one step at a time. This is not a full or complete account, but it definitely depicts a portion of the important ways God protected me and showed His Love in so Many ways even when I didn't see Him.

God still specializes in things that seem impossible and can do what no other power can do. There Is Nothing In Giving Up!!!

www.ingramcontent.com/pod-product-compliance
Lightning Source LLC
Chambersburg PA
CBHW031235120626
46545CB00003B/1125